What Are Friends For?

Dina Santos

Rosen Classroom Books & Materials
New York

1

What are friends for?

Friends help when you
feel afraid.

Friends help when you feel sad.

Friends help when you
feel mad.

Friends make you feel happy.

It is good to have friends!

Words to Know

afraid

happy

mad

sad